TIME TO BE

TIME
TO
BE

Written by

©

authorHOUSE®

AuthorHouse™
1663 Liberty Drive
Bloomington, IN 47403
www.authorhouse.com
Phone: 1-800-839-8640

Published by AuthorHouse   04/25/2013

ISBN: 978-1-4817-8269-2 (sc)
ISBN: 978-1-4817-8268-5 (e)

This book is printed on acid-free paper.

Contents

Introduction

Dear Friends,

Time To Be is a little book of poems with simple ideas to help us all realise that there is perhaps a better way to go through life than we are going right now. We all want happiness and joy in our lives, with fun, laughter and people to love. A world where we all care for one another and help where and when we can, according to our own ideas of how we see ourselves, and what we can do to make it happen.

It is easy in this world today, filled with so much negativity, to think and believe that this is not possible, certainly for us! But we can make a difference, no matter how small. Small, times a few million is a very large small, and that makes a real difference!☺

I've written these poems over a number of years, and they are my way of showing myself that I can do it. I can make a difference, and that if I believe in myself and the Universal Love all around, then everything is possible, and all will be well.

So, take a fresh look at the world, love yourselves for the truly magnificent beings that you are, and go forward in the direction you choose; knowing that anything and everything is possible, and that every event, large or small starts with a single thought, a single step, and before you know it you will have walked a mile . . . .

I wish you all joy and happiness as you take your journey through your life.

In Light and Love

15th May 2007

A Dream of a Better World

Have you, for as long as you can remember had a dream of a better world? A world where all have food, shelter, clothing and perfect abundance in all areas of their lives; a world where everyone lives in peace; a world where all animals are treated with the love and reverence they deserve; a world where all are understood, respected and listened to?

That world is within us. The time is now. Let us open our eyes and see. Then share our vision. Drop our façade. It's time be us. Fully. Completely. Authentically. And what a challenge this can be.

All I can say is thank goodness for the poems in this collection. They are truly inspirational reminding us each day to stay in touch with our inner selves, with Nature, and with God. We are blessed that Helen brought these to us for we are the ones we have been waiting for and it's time to BE.

Wishing you joy as you read.

Zahra Lightway
Sister in the Light".
Lightway Schools

To You From Me

I've been gifted with all these poems you see,
To pass them on so that you and me
Can help this world and all those in it
To be all that we can—for there is no limit.

The words are simple; the message is clear.
It's to live in love and put away fear.
It's to care for the earth and the animals too,
And <u>re</u>-member that's what we're here to do.

It's to bless the world as we make our way through it.
To send out light to all whom we meet.
It's to not be in judgement of all that we see,
For that is not up to you and me.

It's to realise that we are all one
That there is no separation.
That the spark of life that arrived with us
Is the key to all life in the Universe.

It's to tune in with our higher selves
And to live in the multi-verses.
It's to use our eyes so that we are seeing
That we're not Humans Doing—we are Humans BEING.

It's to know in our hearts that we are one.
Separation you know is really no fun,
For it's not the way we're supposed to be—
For **I AM** and **You Are** and so we are **WE!**

© *[signature]*

25th March 2012

18/06/2008

Today Is My Day

Today is my day—it's for me,

It's to open my eyes so that I can see

All the beauty of God that's surrounding me.

If I listen to the universal song in my heart,

Then my day will have a perfect start.

With a heart full of love and an inner fire

I can manifest my every desire.

© *[signature]*

18th June 2006

Invitation From The Heart

Come hither friends and gather round.
Come feel the love that does abound.
For you have never felt like this,
A love that enfolds you in total bliss.

There are no rules that you can break.
There are no mistakes you can make.
For we are learning just like you,
And inviting you all to be a part of this too.

You've all been dreaming of a better place,
Where we're not at war with the human race,
Where all is filled with love and joy.
And there is no difference between girl and boy.

There are no divisions across the nations.
We've not made that a part of our creation.
And we believe and know as you do,
There's no separation between us and you.

Where animals are treated with love and light,
And our reward is companions with eyes so bright.
For they indeed have no need to fear,
For where we are, only love is here.

So come and join us. Help us make it come true,
As we are waiting to be joined by you.
When we're joined together in a world of love
Then we all become **ONE** with the realms above.

© *[signature]*

17th December 2006

To Give Your Life Purpose

To give your life purpose

Just go to your heart,

For this is exactly where you must start.

The truth is inside you

For all that you know

Is written right there

For God told me so.

© _[signature]_

18th June 2006

Blessings

A blessing is something wonderful to do
You see it's good for me and you.

But you must send it out with a heart full of love,
Send it both to here and the realms above.
The Angels will pass them on for you too.
You see Blessings are beautiful things to do.

Send a blessing full of love to a child that cries.
See the light begin to sparkle in those little bright eyes.
See the mother start to smile as the blessing passes on.
See that every little blessing is just like a song.

When you send out a blessing, the world gets brighter.
When you listen to your heart, you will find it
feels lighter
And if you can send a blessing each and every day,
Then you've done your little bit to help others on
their way.

And never ever worry that the blessing may be small
For it's much much better than no blessing at all.

© *signature*

25th October 2005

A New Horizon

What's wrong with us and this world today?
Is there so much going on that we've forgotten how to play?
Have we forgotten how to notice those simple little things
Like the opening of a flower as it trembles in the wind?

To watch the sun come up at dawn its warmth and
light to share.
To show us that the day's begun and that someone
'up there' cares,
To listen to a bird in song as it goes about its day,
To hear it give a warning cry as a cat comes out to play.

To go out in the world each day with an open heart and mind,
To meet each and every person with a thought
that's only kind.
To think the best of all you meet
With a smile on your face, as you go to greet
These people who are just like you, who also have
to see life through.

We must broaden our horizons; we must do so
more each day,
We must put a little time aside so that we may
think and pray.
We must try to do that which we can that will help
to better the lot of man,
For now is the time that we must **DO,**
For your see it's up to **ME** and **YOU.**

©

30th March 1996

Mirror Mirror

When you look into the mirror, tell me what is it you see?
Is it you that you are looking at, or is it really me?
When you look into the mirror and see me standing there,
Am I what you were expecting? Why do you stand and stare?
Do you look me in the eye?
Do you stand there straight and tall?
Or do you gaze right past me and look into the wall?

Tell me, what is it you're frightened of as you sit and gaze at me?
What is it that you cannot face? Is it such a bad reality?
If you look and gaze right past me, what is it that you gain?
Do you think if you ignore it that you'll lessen all the pain?
Do you feel that no one loves you?
Is there nobody that cares?
Must life go on in this sad way; will you go on shedding tears?

So how to change the pattern, how can you put it right?
The first thing that you have to do is let in all the light.
Look in the mirror daily—and do look straight and true.
For only by your doing this will you see the rightful you.
It may seem a little silly, as you gaze into your eyes,
But until you come to know yourself,
how can you then be wise?

So give yourself a moment before you start each day,
And look into the mirror, and be glad you're here today.
And tell yourself that you have faith in you.
That no matter what it takes—you'll see it through,
And you are not afraid to give everything a try,
And that you'll start to live it—not just watch your life go by.

©

21st November 1995

Be True To You

As we go through life, we learn each day
How much worry and strife is on the way.
The weather is grey and the wind is strong
And we think—"where on earth did we go wrong"?

Is it really so hard for us to be good?
Why is it thought sissy to do as we should?
Does it hurt to do a kindness a day
And help another person along the way?

To give someone a smile instead of a frown,
Lift someone up—not knock them down.
Lend a shoulder to cry on—wipe away a tear,
Take a little time to listen with a friendly ear.

Tell your family you love them, tell your friends as well
See their eyes light up with joy.
Welcome in that baby who is a girl—
Even though you wanted a boy.

Do the best you can—not just make do.
Put the effort in and see it through.
For it doesn't matter what the others think
Let them laugh and jeer—it is they who will sink.

Have belief in yourself so that you can say

**"I FEEL GOOD, I FEEL GLAD,
I'VE MADE NO ONE FEEL BAD—
AND I'M PROUD OF WHAT I DID TODAY!"**

©

8th May 1996

A Prayer For Strength

Give me the strength to face this day
and all those in it.

Give me the calmness of mind to do my work,
and let me find joy in it.

Give me serenity and purpose to last
throughout the day.

Give me love and joy and laughter
to point me in the way.

Give me patience and forbearance,
so that I may see this through.

And I thank you, 'cause I know,
you'll give me your love too.

©

March 1996

The Heart & Home

The evening is a friendly time to go out for a walk,
For people are all slowing down after a hard days' work;
And though the homeward bound cars are still noisy,
And overhead the planes are coming in,
The earth itself is feeling warm and lazy,
And the people are at home all settled in.

It's time for us to sit back and relax now
Away from all the noises and the din.
To take a breath and calm our weary bodies,
And let the warmth and love of home seep in.

This is the time for mellow contemplation
Of the things we've done today, both right and wrong.
To look with joy and peace upon our loved ones
For whom, with love, we labour on and on.

To sit in quiet peaceful meditation,
And let the worries of the day go by,
And tell ourselves that, despite confrontation,
We won through the day by holding our heads high!

Now the time has come to join in with our children,
And talk about the highlights of their day.
To brush their shiny hair and wipe away a tear,
'Cause someone wouldn't let them stop and play.

It's time now for those lovely hugs and kisses,
As sleepy heads on tired shoulders roll.
To carry them upstairs—and listen to their prayers,
And tuck them in so to dreamland they can go.

This is the time of day that is the best you see,
For at this time you're safe at home and with your family.

©

30th August 1995

22/05/2010

Spring Is Near

Do I detect a little light
As I wake up now each day?
Shall I dare to even think perhaps
That Spring is on the way?

For I won't be sad to see the last
Of these dull days we've had,
And when Spring does truly reach us
I am sure we'll all be glad!

Oh what a joy it will surely be
To wake to a shining sun
And a blue sky and the birds' cry
Yes . . . Spring will surely come!

© [signature]

27th February 1995

Beware

The common is a natural area where hazards do occur from time
to time (sign on local common near my home)

You may not enter here for this piece of God's good land belongs
to me—not you.

And you cannot go to there—not unless you've paid the fare.
And it's really not allowed that you should merely
stand and stare.
And although a smile costs nothing, what you
get is just a glare . . .
Is this now the world we live in?
Tell me if you think it's fair . . .
And I thought the world was here for all of us to share.

When God made this lovely place for us to live in
And created all the beauty that we see.
He didn't say that we should not be let in
He meant it for our use—yes you AND me.

He meant us all to live in peace together
To help each other out along the way.
To laugh and sing and wander through the heather.
To love him and to say a prayer each day.

He gave our planet lungs that we might breathe
And as you know, for this we need the trees.
But we cut them down so fast that our atmosphere
can't last
And very soon we'll all be on our knees.

For we've forgotten how to take account of nature
To accept that it's important in our lives.
And that every little creature has its special part
to play,
To enable this dear world of ours to carry on each day.

But we decimate it everywhere we wander,
As wherever we go nature comes out worst.
For when we build a dam to divert water,
There is somewhere else that will now die of thirst.

I think the time has come now—
There is something we MUST face
The only thing creating this, is US—
The Human Race.

© *[signature]*

17th August 1998

War Is Not An Option

It's not a solution
It breeds revolution
It angers the ordinary man in the street.

We don't want to fight
Except for the right
To be friends with all whom we meet.

When you're in the position
To make these decisions
Remember just who you are sending to die.

They are not a resource
But individual beings
Just exactly like you and I.

© *[signature]*

19th February 2003

Falling

Did you ever get the feeling that you're falling,
And you cannot seem to stop what's going on.
That the days and weeks pass by in the blinking
of an eye?
And you realise how quickly time does fly.

Can it really be the year is halfway over
That spring has gone and summer nearly passed?
And still you keep on falling, and now you start to think,
That it's time you took complete control at last.

You stop yourself from racing ever forward,
So you have time to think and plan ahead.
It's not so much you mind that the time has
passed you by,
It's just you want to know where you are lead!

You have to find the time to sit and think now,
To take the path that is the one for you,
Not just to let the life you live take over,
Which we all know is what it tends to do.

So sit and take a moment.
Let your heart and mind attune,
And give yourself the time you need
To do what's right for you.

© [signature]

3rd February 1998

It's A Wonderful World

I marvel at all nature.
I love to be outside
In any kind of weather
Morning noon and eventide.

To wake up in the morning
To the sound of singing birds,
And the dawns glow,
And the cock's crow,
Oh . . . to put in into words . . . !

I love a really heavy wind
With just a touch of rain
To blow away the cobwebs
That circle round my brain.

And I laugh to see the squirrels
As they run both up and down,
And try so hard to remember
Where they stored their nuts in the ground!

To lie down in a grassy field
Is another of life's joys.
To watch the birds upon the wing
As they spiral in the skies.

I love to hear a baby laugh
A great big joyous chuckle,
As it sucks upon your finger,
Or chews upon a knuckle.

It's A Wonderful World . . . . / 2

It waves its feet up in the air,
For it has just discovered,
It's got some lovely wiggly toes
Right there under the covers!

To see a sunny dimpled face,
And hear the joy and laughter—
The sort of sound that makes you think
Of happy ever after.

There are so many things to love,
So many sights to see,
And I thank the Lord just every day
That he made it possible for me.

© *[signature]*

10th August 1995

Keep On Keeping On

Sometimes I wonder what to do,
in order to make my dreams come true,
To make things happen seems to need so much,
Do I really have the magic touch?
The effort required is great you see.
So I think to myself, is this for me?

Can I continue on this way?
What makes it all worthwhile?
Then something tiny happens, someone gives me a smile.
It's such a little thing you think,
but it doesn't make my spirits sink.
And suddenly the sun is out as I laugh and sing
and run about.

And what a difference it does make.
My day is now much brighter.
As I carry on with the work of the day.
My heart is so much lighter.

So I know I need not worry about those dreams of mine,
For if I just keep on keeping on, then all will turn out fine.

© *[signature]*

22nd January 1996

Spreading The Light

I spread the Light
So everyone can see.
I spread the Light
To show we're near to Thee.

I spread the Light
So everyone can know,
That to be so near to Thee
Is what gives this inner glow.

I spread the Light
So that everyone will be
Enfolded in this Light
Which comes direct from Thee.

20th August 2006

Dreams

As I walk along the road, what do I see?
I see a lot of people just like me,
With hopes and fears and dreams to ponder,
And isn't the world we live in a wonder?

To travel the world the wonders to see,
To fly like a bird or buzz like a bee,
To ski down a mountain that I have just climbed,
To learn to communicate with those who are blind.

To listen to music, perhaps play it too,
To write a small poem, and read it to you.
To paint with the eye of one who can see
How much this beauty means to me.

Oh yes, I could wonder and dream the whole day
Just watching the children and people at play.
And right from my heart to Thee I will pray,
And give thanks for the joy of today.

©

29th February 1996

Have You Ever Wondered—
Did You Know? . . . .

That when it snows, your nose and hands will glow?
And how was I to know, I mean now think,
That if I chose the short straw I could not finish my drink?
And have you ever wondered when
something goes astray,
And turns up three days later—just where it went to stay?

That what is black and white and read all over,
Is a newspaper—quite clear for all to see
But when it's said and sounds like "red"—it's not so easy.
With this language you can have great difficulty!

That bow and bough which sound alike don't look
the same on paper,
That listen has a silent "t"; psychology starts with a "p"!
and "i" comes always before "e"—excepting
when it's after "c"!
My goodness what is going on? What's happening to me?

No wonder that we all go round in circles,
For we seem to whirl much faster every day.
And the spinning makes us dizzy, and we fear that
we might drop,
And we turn around and scream that we want the
world to stop . . . . !

I long just for a simple life that's free of all these fears,
A place of joy and laughter without the need for tears.
And I know that this is possible, but we must do our part,
And live not from the mind at all—but only from the heart

©

25th January 1997

Thank You Lord For This Beautiful Day

Thank you Lord for this beautiful day.
For the birds and trees—for these I pray.
For the sun in the sky and the wind in my face,
All served with love and light and grace.

For the sun shining down like a glittering ray
Which gives us strength to face the day.
For the song of the birds and the buzz of the bees,
And the squirrels that scamper in the trees.

For the chance to BE—and the eyes to see
Are all more reasons for thanking Thee,
And as I go through the day today,
I lift up my heart and to Thee I pray,

For strength and patience, love of course too
To do those things that I must do.
And Lord if for any reason I should stray.
Help me try again the very next day!

©

16th July 1997

Turning Dark Into Light

I do not see a world that is dark and grey.
I see a world basking in the sun's rays.

I do not see a world of toil and strife.
I see a world full of joy and life.

I do not see a world unjust and unfair.
I see a world where everyone shares.

I do not see a world full of hate and spite.
I see a world full of love and light.

I do not see a world that is falling apart,
I see a world now ruled by the heart.

I do not see a world in which hate alone lives,
I see a world where everyone forgives.

I do not see a world that is always at war.
I see a world full of open doors.

I do not see a world full of lust and greed
I see a world where nobody needs.

I do not see a world that is dark as night.
I see a world moving forward into light.

I do not see a world that is arid and dry.
I see a world so beautiful it makes me cry.

Turning Dark Into Light . . . / 2

I do not see a world that I must fear.
I see a world where only love is there.

I do not see a world coming to an end.
I see a world that is starting to ascend.

I do not see the world as it is today.
For loving the whole world will take all that away.

© *[signature]*

29th August 2005

A Day Dream

Have you ever been so tired that you cannot quite recover
The energy that is required to put one foot in front
of the other?
The mind is gone and it no longer thinks,
The more tired that you get the deeper do you sink;
A lethargy steals over you and your eyes they slowly close
And your head drops ever closer as you doze.

When every muscle that you have is still,
And cannot move without, an outpouring of will.
And you lazily just lie there in the middle of both worlds.
Neither here and neither there but that wondrous
place within,
The Land of Dreams.

Where everything is just the way it should be,
The weather it is perfect, light and bright.
The people are all friendly, there is not a foe in sight
And everywhere you look is sheer delight.

Where animals are free and rightly treated
And people they are happy all around.
And although there is an element of noise about the place,
That all of it just has a happy sound.

There are no strident voices nor no sirens
And people are not rushing everywhere.
The pace is just as fast as you may want it
And you can see all round you signs of care.

A Day Dream . . . . / 2

Where flowers and the trees are in abundance,
The grass is greener than you've seen before,
And your eyes are open wide at all the colours that you see.
In vast arrays, and every kind, and some you've never seen.
And song is in the air and all creatures great and small
Are milling all about and they have no fear at all—
And you are standing there now straight and tall.

You wander round in total relaxation
As you drink in all the splendour that you see.
And although you know you must return to where
you were before
I hope that you've enjoyed your visit here to me.
So come again and see me—won't you please?

© *Helen*

Summer 1996

Wondering

I wonder what it's like to be
As free as a bird or a bumblebee,
To float as the clouds do in the sky,
To ripple like the grass when the wind passes by.

To shout out loud and drown the thunder,
To watch the lightning with awe and wonder,
As it looks as though it splits the sky,
When the dark and roiling clouds race by.

To fly on the wing as an eagle rare,
To run like a hound that is chasing a hare,
To climb a mountain like a goat,
That has no need of axe or rope,

To see the world from outer space,
It really is an incredible place.
To be like an ant as it scurries around,
And carries such weight which does astound.

There are so many wondrous things
That God has made that make me sing,
And I hold to my heart the joy and love
That totally surrounds me from the realms above.

© *[signature]*

9th February 1998

Imagination

Imagination is a wonderful thing,
It has no boundaries, it has no strings.
It can take you to a place where your heart can sing.
Yes, Imagination is a wonderful thing.

Imagination can be a joy to all
In your darkest hour it can stop a fall.
No matter where or what or who,
There is NOTHING your Imagination cannot do.

Imagination is the way to go.
You can be there in a flash or take it slow.
You can swim in the ocean; interact with the fish,
You can be the top chef and invent a new dish.

You can climb a mountain till you reach the top.
You can run forever and never stop . . .
Why do we worry what is going on around,
When we have the Universe as our playing ground?

Yes . . . . Imagination is a wonderful thing.

© *signature*

28th May 2005

Who Is This Friend?

Who is this friend that comes to call,

Who fills my heart with light,

To whom with love I give my all?

He is my hearts delight.

I love him as I love no other.

Whatever he asks it is no bother.

For everything is asked with love

When the message comes from above.

2002-2003

A Sense Of Fun

I've seen a boat sailing in the sky,

The shape of a cloud as it passes by.

I've seen a bird swim in the sea,

And a fish that flies, oh goodness me!

This is not normal we would say,

But God made these. It is his way.

To show he has a sense of fun,

Another way that we are one!

© *[signature]*

9th September 2002

I Love The Wind

I love the wind upon my face.

I love to watch the great clouds race

Across a bright blue sunny sky,

A gentle way to watch time fly!

© *signature*

2002-2003

Teach Me

Teach me Lord to know thy ways.

Let me pray to you each and every day.

Give me the heart to carry on.

Let me always be filled with songs,

That speak of love and joy and laughter,

And I will love you forever after.

© *[signature]*

28 November 2002

Time To Play

"Hello Mummy". "Hello Daddy."
"Is it nearly time for tea?
Have you got a little time now,
So that you can play with me?"

"You hadn't time this morning,
'Cause you had to go to work,
And the house it needed cleaning,
And the dog needed a walk."

"Then your friend came in for coffee,
And you had to stop and chat,
And you didn't want me joining in.
There was no time after that."

"Then we had to do the shopping,
'Cause you hadn't bought our food.
And I really, really did my best,
And I tried so hard to be good."

"And I wanted so to help you,
When at last we got back home,
For I knew that you would need some help,
If you wanted to get done."

"But you didn't want my help then,
'Cause you hadn't got the time,
But the fact that you were all behind
Was not a fault of mine."

Time To Play . . . / 2

"Why can't you play with me now?
For I've waited all day long,
And I really need a cuddle and a kiss,
But you have not the time to give me this."

"Hello Mummy," "Hello Daddy."
"Can I please go out to play?
'Cause I know you have no time left
To play with me today."

© *[signature]*

16th January 1998

27/02/2008

In A Hurry

Runners running.
Bikers biking.
Hikers hiking.
Everyone one is in the flow.
Do they know which way to go?

No time to sit. No time to lie.
No time to watch the world go by.
Rushing here, rushing there.
We are rushing everywhere.

To what purpose?
To what end?
Have you time to make a friend?

Have you time to watch the sky
And see the clouds as they float on by?
Watch the birds upon the wing?
Stop and listen as they start to sing?

Let the sun shine on your face.
You really do not need to race
From here to there, and hither and yon.
Just stop and sit a while—go on!

©

1st February 2004

Believe

God says it all depends you see
Upon the way you look at me.
For you are taught to fear all things
This is not right, your heart should sing.

The essence of the world is love
For each and every thing.
It matters not their colour or shape
What counts is found within.

A loving heart is all you need.
An unswerving belief that you will succeed
In everything you choose to do.

Go on—believe—make it come true!

© *[signature]*

15th March 2001

Have No Fear

"My dearest children have no fear,
For know that I am always near.
Just step into your heart to see
How near I am to thee.

You do not have to travel,
Or go away from home,
For I am always with you
You are never left alone.

So gather up your strength now
And go about your day,
And know forever in your heart,
I am only a thought away."

© *[signature]*

28th November 2004

29/01/2005

God Bless This Bright & Sunny Day

God Bless this bright and sunny day.
God bless the path that shows the way.

God Bless the cobwebs that I break,
As across the common my walk I take.

God Bless the birds and all the trees.
God bless the all life-giving breeze.

God bless the sun and wind and rain,
Making rainbows through my window pane.

God bless us all that we may see,
And in that seeing, be near Thee.

2000

Be Me

Play is something we should do—yes me and you!

Work is not a must you see—we must be free!

The reason we're here is quite simple you see.

We are here <u>not</u> to do—but to BE!

This doing is not all it's cracked up to BE!

For whilst we are DOING—we cannot be free.

And I have discovered most importantly,

That it really is time to BE ME!

© *[signature]*

12th April 2004

Beloved Friend

Fill me with your love divine.
Give me the strength I know to be mine.
Let my mind be clear and my thoughts be true,
So that when it is time, I can come to you.

Let me show all those who wish to see
How easy it is to be with Thee.
For there is nothing we need to do
In order to be with you.

For you are with us in all that we do.
You are in our hearts—in the centre is you.
We are never alone. We are never apart,
For we are joined heart to heart.

I have no fear of the death to come,
For I know in my heart that we are one.
And when my journey here is complete,
I will fly to you with wings on my feet.

And I know that whatever I have done,
You and I will still be one.

© *[signature]*

16th May 2006

Living In Fear

You live in fear,

You die in fear,

You are hardly aware that you are here.

Come look at the world.

It is both bright and gay.

You really are <u>not</u> meant to live life this way.

© *[signature]*

19th March 2003

I Am The Light

I am the Light.
I shine the Light.
I am Love.
I am wise.
There is no disguise.

I am Me.
I am You.
I help you see it through.
I am for You.
You are for Me.
Together we shall **SEE.**

I take your hand.
You take mine,
And we'll go forth together
In this moment of Time

To do what we can,
To be who we are,
Universal beings of Love,
As we follow our star.

©

4th March 2007

Always—All Ways

I am Me as I'll always be
—doing my best to be Me.

I am free as I'll always be
—totally free to be me.

I am in God as I'll always be
—as he is always in me.

I have no fear as God is near
—for he is all ways here.

I love God and he loves me
Now THAT IS the way to be.

© *[signature]*

16th June 2005

Wispy White Clouds

Wispy white clouds and a pale blue sky
Lazily watching as life passes by.

Windswept leaves and bits of paper
Leafless trees—the winter side of nature.

A peacefulness, even though it's busy
A sort of hazy hum in the middle of the city.

A seat in the park on a winter's day
Watching and listening as the wind and leaves play.

A perfect place just to sit for a moment
And give thanks to God for today.

© _[signature]_

16th June 2005

We Are One

I wanted to find this place within me,
Which is the place from where I'd see
Just where I'm meant to be.

I wanted to find just where to go,
Should I go fast, should I go slow?
I really needed to know.

I walked and walked, I sat and stared.
I ran, I shouted—I was full of fear.
Was there no one with whom to share?

I cried to God "What can it be?
What is it that I cannot see?"
He said *"My child it's Me"*

"You race around timed by the clock.
Your doors should be open but they are locked,
Would you hear me if I knocked?"

"Can't you feel me in the sights and sounds
And the awesome beauty that is all around,
And the life which does abound?"

"I am with you in everything you do.
I am there to help you see it through
For I am part of YOU."

"My love for you it has no bounds.
No restrictions are attached you see
To my love for thee
For YOU are part of ME"

"If you look around with eyes that are clear,
My child, you will see me everywhere.
I am in the rain, I am in the sun,
I play with you too as you're having fun."

"FOR YOU AND I ARE ONE."

© *[signature]*

22 August 2001

Learn To Love Me

A golden way upon which to walk
The golden path as we learn to talk.
A way that is filled with love and joy,
As all our senses we learn to employ.

The scent of a rosc on a gentle breeze,
The rustle of leaves on a large plane tree.
The touch of the sun upon your face.
This world is really a beautiful place.

So use your eyes the wonders to see,
And in that seeing learn to love me.

© *[signature]*

9th May 2006

Doubts

Why do you doubt yourselves so much?
Do I not heal with my loving touch?
Can't you feel me all around
Like stereophonic sound?

I am with you wherever you may go,
Whether you travel fast or slow.
No matter it takes months or days,
I am with you always—**ALL WAYS**.

© *[signature]*

28th November 2004

Prayer To The Angels

Beloved Friends help me through this day.

Let me not panic.

Let me not fear.

Let me just love all those who are near.

Let me be happy.

Let me be gay.

Let me give others a chance for their say.

Let me just **BE** for the rest of the day

In this Moment of **NOW**—where I'll stay.

29th April 2005

Rainbow

A rainbow dancing across the sky

Brings joy to the heart and a gleam in the eye,

For it makes a bridge from the earth to the sky,

And we'll travel on that when we say "goodbye"

© *Helen*

2002-2003

Freedom From Fear

Freedom from fear is here.

The only thing to fear is fear itself.

So right now put your fear on the shelf.

Mark it cancelled. Mark it done,

For now your battle with fear is won.

Each time you think it may be back,

Just immediately give it the sack!

©

16th June 2005

We Are Under Attack

(After the bombings in London 11.7.05)

We are under attack, attack, attack!
Keep on moving—do not look back!
Do not panic, do not fear
Remember that God and the Angels are here.

It's a wake-up call that we've been given
For too long now we have let ourselves be driven.
Remember who it is that put the people in power
We can't just keep on hiding in our little bower.

Horrific though it is, we are the creators
of this way of life that we're living now.
It is time to move on, not be couch potatoes
Stand up, be counted, start making a vow.

That we will not stand aside and let it happen
We can cure the world of its worries and cares.
All it takes is the action of a positive vibe.
So that we can all continue to be alive.

We must live our lives with love for one another,
We must love all we meet as a sister or a brother.
It does not matter which religion or creed
For we all originate from the very same seed.

There must be no revenge for it is not sweet
It propagates more fighting—perhaps in your street.
We must really turn our lives around so we can stand and say
"To the best of our ability, we helped the world today".

© *[signature]*

12th July 2005

Fill Your Heart With Love

Fill your heart with love.
Fill your mind with song.
Think only of right and never of wrong.
Think of good not bad.
Think of happy not sad,
For then, you can only be glad.

Think Peace not war.
Open that closed door,
And talk with those that you meet.
Go forth with a smile,
For this can beguile,
And give everyone a treat.

Don't put someone down.
Don't greet with a frown,
For the sky will seem cloudy not bright.
All you need to do
Is be true to you,
And go forth in Love and Light.

© *[signature]*

9th November 2006

Wishing

The sun is shining bright today.
I don't want to be here I want to play.
I want to walk beneath the sky,
To stand and watch as the birds fly by,
To see as they soar upon the wing,
The sight of which makes me want to sing.

I want to watch as the clouds float by
Making wonderful shapes up there in the sky.
Some snowy white, some black as thunder,
I stand and look and am full of wonder.
Some lined with silver, some with gold,
On their beauty I am totally sold.

I could lie on the grass and gaze all day.
I think this is a wonderful way to play.

© *Helen*

7th February 2001

Why Did I Wait So Long

Why did I wait 'till now in life
To sort out all my woes and strife?
Even knowing it's what I should do,
Why did I wait so long?

Why did I wait so long to see
By not allowing my eyes to see,
What it is in life that I **can** be?
Why did I wait so long?

Why do I not say what I mean
But put up this amazing screen?
Then look through it with blinkered eyes,
And only then do I realise,
This barrier it comes from me!
That's why I cannot see!

Happiness **is** meant for me.
Abundance so I can be free.
For all those things I want to do,
I will not wait so long.

I will not wait another day,
But get down on my knees and pray
To God from whom all Blessings flow,
Who says "**Don't wait—just GO!**"

© _Helen_

18th September 2005

Learning

Dear Lord, I am learning to know Thee.

I have lifted my eyes so that I can see

The glory of you shining all around me.

I am working so hard to be what I can,

And I do my best to give a helping hand,

And I know this is right for I feel it too,

As it's bringing me ever closer to you.

© *Helen*

28th July 2006

So Much Love

So much love enfolds me.
So much love I feel.
How can I not accept the fact
That you are very real?

You are in the air, the sun, the sea.
You are in the birds and in every tree.
You are in the sky and in the land,
For they were created by your dear hand.

Forgive me Lord for being obtuse,
And thinking I am off little use.
For You are Me, and I am You.
There ARE many things I CAN do!

©

6th January 2005

Shine Your Light On Me

Beloved Spirit, shine your light on me.
Let it be only Peace that I see.
Let me join with those who want this too,
So that we may be nearer to You.

Let there be no fear.
Let there be no fright.
Let us pray for Peace with all our might.
Let the fighting stop.
Let the World be still.
Let it be only Peace that we Will.

Let our minds be full of Peace and Love.
Let us live on the earth as you do above.
Let us fill our hearts with Love Divine,
So that we are truly of One Great Mind.

Let us see with your eyes.
Let us feel with your heart.
Let us fill ourselves with Love.
And when we are ready, Oh Beloved Spirit,
Let us join with you up above.

For I want to heal this earth of mine.
I want to join the Love Divine.
I want my life on this earth to be free.
So that I am One with Thee.

© Helen

29th October 2006

Angels Are Everywhere

People are so wonderful the brave things that they do.
They'll risk their very lives each day
So they can rescue you.

It could be on a mountain, it could be out at sea,
Or maybe something simple as a cat, stuck in a tree

Whatever the occasion that led to this event,
Remember that whoever comes Is surely "heaven sent".

They give their all to help us. They ask for nothing more
than to have been of service, so you are safe once more.

It makes me feel so humble when I have asked to see
One of the many Angels who are always helping me.

For I realise we do see them as we go along our way,
For they're the wonderful beings who rescue us each day.

So do not judge the people that you pass by each day
For one of them might be the one
Who'll rescue YOU today!

© *[signature]*

7th July 2006

Oneness

Go before me throughout this day.
Show me, show me, keep showing the way.
For I'm a little lost now, I have just missed the path.
Show me, show me, show me, so I can be with you at last.

Icy white cold mountains, glistening in the sun,
Almost touching the clouds, and straining towards the One.
I'm on my journey upward, ever higher do I seek
To climb this glistening mountain and stand there
on the peak.
I hold my hands up to the sky, and lift my head up
oh so high,
And speak to you, heart open wide, just as I am—
nothing to hide.

I'm climbing, yes I'm climbing, I'm reaching for the top.
And know beloved Teacher that I will never stop.
So wait for me, I'm coming, no matter what it takes,
For if you've got the patience, I know I'll not be late,
To take my place upon that peak, and join the Oneness
that I seek.

© *Helen*

15th February 2008

Nearer To Thee

Dear Lord, from whom all blessings flow,
From you 'up above' to us below.
I ask that you do shine on me,
So you, I can clearly see.

Open my eyes, so that I will see
Just what I must do to be near thee.
Unblock my ears so that I will hear
All those words of yours I hold so dear.

Clear my mind of negativity.
Take away the fear that parts you from me.
Fill my heart with love, so that I may be
Ever, and all ways, nearer to thee.

© *[signature]*

March 2003

Beloved Voice Within Me

Beloved voice within me sing unto my heart,
Open my ears with your loving voice
Tell me again that I have a choice.
My life is mine to do as I please
Not let just anyone lead.

Beloved spirit stay by my side
I am standing here heart open wide.
For I long with my heart and know it's true
That all I want is to be near you.

© *TWebb*

4th December 2002

Smile

If you smile with your heart in your eyes,

They will reflect the stars in the sky.

A feeling of warmth will spread right through

Letting you know it's the right thing to do.

Laugh with a joy that has no bounds.

Sing out and raise your voice up high,

For nothing pleases more than sounds

Of joy and laughter reaching the sky.

©

April 2006

04/12/2005

I Am A Tree

I am a tree just look at me.

I give you air, I give you shade

I give you life

Why do you decimate me?

I am your lungs I give you breath.

I shelter birds in me they nest.

I care for them and they care too.

Why do you maim me—what have I done to you?

©

2005

Nearer To You

Give me the patience that I lack.
Let me not shout, let me pat on the back.
Let me find the good in all that I see,
So that I may be nearer to Thee.

Let me not judge no matter what.
Let me be happy with what I have got.
Let me not wish for all those things
That don't true happiness bring.

Let me be happy all the while.
Let me greet every day with a great big smile.
Let me find true joy in all that I do,
So that I will be nearer to **YOU.**

© *[signature]*

December 2002

Loving From The Heart Centre

Calmness is a state of mind.
In this state of calm, you are always kind.
For you are not worried, and you are not stressed,
And you don't end up in a terrible mess.

If you can stay calm and in your centre,
There are no doors that you cannot enter.
The road is clear. The path is free,
And then you have time just to **BE.**

To Be what you want and do what you can
That is good for you and also for man.
It doesn't have to be big, it doesn't have to be grand.
It's just giving someone a smile and a helping hand.

For no matter how small, if you give your all,
And you've done it with a heart full of love,
Then the Angels will give a clarion call,
And surround you from the realms above.

© *[signature]*

14th October 2005

Time To Celebrate

It's time for us to celebrate
This time of Christmas cheer.
A time for us to give out thanks
For the bounty of the year.

We've lost our way a little bit,
And turned it into "What'll I get"?
The meaning is now quite obscure
And presents are the only lure.

So let us change the way of things,
And not just worry what Christmas brings.
Let us raise our voices and with our hearts sing
To the Glory of God and the joy that he brings.

Let us join our hands together in prayer.
Let us ring this world with love divine.
Let us send out love to **ALL** who are here.
Then surely we can join as one great mind.

If we work on this we can feed the world.
We can find all those who are lost.
We can rebuild homes and lives as well
With total love as the only cost.

Let's not have another year, as we've had before,
When only a few can pass through the door.
If we open our hearts and still our minds,
We will realise we are all one kind.

So let us intend with hearts so true
To do all we can, so both me and you
Can help the world and everyone in it,
To be all that they can, for there is no limit.

© *signature*

20th November 2006

O God Of Love

O God of Love!

O God of Joy!

My love is overflowing.

I look to You and my heart is full,

And my inner soul is glowing.

© *[signature]*

28th November 2004

Wait & See

I will survive.
Through the trouble and the strife
I'll live my life.

I have control.
When something new comes in to view
I will enrol.

I will get by.
I will do it all in Truth
I will not lie.

I have myself,
And I have you
And together we'll see it through.

I'll take the ups as well as downs.
Greet with a smile not with a frown.
I'll say "I have"
I will be **ME**
YOU WAIT AND SEE!

2005

My Heart Is Light

My heart is light and I'm full of fire,
I begin to see all that I desire.
I set my mind, let my ego go,
And concentrate being in the flow,
And tell myself—JUST GO!

Don't wait around for the perfect time.
Don't worry whether you'll make a dime.
Think what you've always wanted to do,
And take steps to make your dreams come true.
There is nothing else you need to do.

Put your faith in God and the Universe too.
For they are there to help you through.
You have but to ask, whatever the task,
And the answer will come to you.

ISN'T LIFE WONDERFUL? ☺

© *[signature]*

18th January 2009

Tune In To Your Heart Centre

There is a beautiful universe and world out there and we are all an integral part of it.

Let's explore it with our hearts and minds in openness and peace.

Be happy, joyful, compassionate and, above all, loving in thought, word and deed, to each and every sentient living entity, animal, human and of nature, on the earth.

Let us go forth to see and experience all that we can, both in our minds and physically. Just remember that every thought, every action and every smile, helps the world go round, and we will all be doing our part to make a truly beautiful and wondrous world.

We are so very Blessed to have such an awesome world to live in.

In Love and Light

© *signature*

23rd April 2013

Connecting With Your Angels

Did you know that we all have our own very special Angels as well as all the Archangels and Masters of the Universe! Wow! What a thought! Would you like to connect with your Angels?

Sit down quietly where you won't be interrupted. Decide which Angel you wish to connect with i.e. your Guardian Angel, your house Angel, (there are Angels for literally everything). Take a few deep calm breaths and say "Beloved Guardian Angel please tell me your name" Do not think, just let the name come into your mind—whatever the name is, it will be the correct one. You will then be able to connect daily with your Guardian Angel. Once you have done this you will be amazed at what a difference it makes to your life. In acknowledging the presence of your Angel you will become aware of one marvellous fact—you will know that **YOU ARE NEVER ALONE!** Now isn't that a really nice feeling? ☺

Of course you can speak to your Angel in any way you wish. There are no set rules of how to do this. I am only giving you an example. But please treat your Angel as your best friend and talk to them naturally. They do most certainly have a sense of humour!

Now, as you know, God gave us all free will, and the Angels cannot interfere as this is not allowed. To get their assistance you merely have to ASK them, and believe me, they are waiting right there hoping against hope that you will ask them to help and guide you. It is their heart's desire to help and assist you. However, you can only ask them if your requests are for the highest good of yourself, everyone else and the Universe. They cannot assist you to do harm in any way, anyway.

You can now talk to your Angels and ask them to help you with anything and everything. Can't find your keys, send a thought to your Angel and you will suddenly know where you left them. You are worried about something, give the worry to your Angel. They will help. Oh yes, it does work. Every morning I say Hi to my house Angel, and Bye and Hello when I come back. My home is never empty!

So make yourself some new friends today—introduce yourself to your Angels. ☺

2012

Stress Busting—
With No Pills, Potions Or Psychiatrists!

It's easy. No drugs. No travelling to sit on a couch! Not expensive—only the cost of paper. Re-use old paper with space on it. Use up that old notebook with a few pages left at the end. Be kind to the planet!

If you are feeling stressed, angry, frustrated or any of these things, just grab some paper and a pen.

Go and sit quietly, or do it in bed, and literally—just write. Turn your mind off and just write anything and everything that comes into your mind. Don't worry about sentences, punctuation or anything like that. It also doesn't matter about being able to read it afterwards. I would suggest that this is totally not necessary. The reason you are writing is to get all these thoughts and frustrations out of your mind and on to the paper! Just totally let go and keep going until you realise that you have totally run out of things to write. This can sometimes be pages long. It doesn't matter. Just keep going.

When you have finished, relax for a few minutes, and you will find that your mood has totally changed. You no longer have a mind that is churning away. It is calm, and you are calm. You feel so much better. It amazes me just how effective this is. You are literally clearing your mind and putting it on the paper.

Now, all you have to do is either tear the paper up very small, or burn it. You really don't want to read it. It is done. It is gone, and you are now ready to face the world.

Have a relaxing bath or shower. Listen to your favourite music, and just delight in your feeling of peace.

Do this anytime you feel like it. I hope that you find this as effective as I have done. I think one day I wrote 7 foolscap pages!! I think I must have been a mite fed up that day! ☺

God Bless and enjoy your life.

©

2012

Affirmations

Affirmations are sayings we use to create our dreams and bring all that we desire to help us in our lives. One of course, is that we all deserve abundance. Now Abundance does not just mean money. It can be joy, love, health, romance, self-esteem, job success and a life released from resentment and pain. Opportunities are everywhere. We have unlimited choices:

"I am an unlimited Being accepting from an unlimited source in an unlimited way".

"I am open and receptive to receiving my abundance from expected and unexpected sources."

This allows you to receive your abundance in any way. You are not limiting yourself to, say receiving from a friend, or a recently departed relative!

Over the next few pages, I have given you some examples of affirmations that you can use. Tune into your heart and ask "What is it I need to learn today that is for my highest good?". Then make up an affirmation for it e.g. "Today I am love. I choose to be love and show love to everyone I meet".

You can use affirmations for absolutely every situation. Affirmations can be said in your mind, out loud and also when you are doing your mirror work.

Affirmations . . . / 2

Do not put out any negative thoughts. You may ask for anything and everything, *"ask and it shall be given to you"*. Your intentions must be clear and positive. It is no good asking for something and then immediately thinking "I will never get that" "it won't happen" etc. because of course, it won't happen. In fact as everything that you would like or desire is already there waiting for you, you must give thanks and be in gratitude.

You are wanting to move or change your job, say "thank you for my new job, perfect for me and my highest good". Also "thank you for my new home. Perfect for my needs, in wonderful natural surroundings, with friendly neighbours and beautiful views"—just anything you desire. Then you must leave it to your angels to give you what you desire. Do not put any restrictions, let the Angels help you.

©

2012

Affirmations—make up your own

❖ *I release all resistance to money and I now allow it to flow joyously into my life.*

❖ *Today I create happiness for myself and those around me.*

❖ *Today I will send a Blessing to all that I meet and those on my train.*

Affirmations 2

- ❖ *God Bless this day and all the wonderful things it will bring.*

- ❖ *I am grateful for all the love in my life.*

- ❖ *I spread Light wherever I am.*

Affirmations/Special Thoughts For Today

Write down any special thoughts and or intuition that comes to you throughout the day. Points that suddenly are the answer to thoughts you may have been thinking, or "wow" moments when something suddenly makes sense.

Keep a note book handy, and one by your bed. These are invaluable.

Mirror Work

As my poem says, this is a very empowering thing to do. It really does allow you to be in your own power.

To start mirror work you really have to be able to look yourself in the eyes and tell yourself that you love you just the way you are i.e. I say "Helen I love you just the way you are" and repeat this a total of three times.

You may find, at first, that you look everywhere except at yourself. You may even feel a little bit silly, but it really doesn't take long to get used to this. The idea behind this is that you must learn to love yourself. If you don't, how can you expect anyone else to love you? This empowers you to feel so much better about yourself, you have to see and acknowledge that you are a perfect Being, there is nothing wrong with you, and that God loves you exactly as you are right now.

Once you have tuned in to yourself, then you further empower yourself with affirmations.

"I am full of light and power my energy is growing higher".
I am an unlimited Being accepting from an unlimited source, in an unlimited way".
"I am Divine Peace, I am Divine Joy, I am Divine Love".

Say as many affirmations and prayers as well if you wish to. When you feel you have done enough, you close by saying the same words as at the beginning. Do this every morning; it is a very good way to start the day. You will feel connected and in tune with your inner self, and find that you will go to work with a smile on your face, and one smile begets another from your fellow travellers—a much nicer and happier way to start the day!

As you get used to doing this you may be able to see the light/power gathering around your head, this gives you a real feeling of joy. Have a wonderful time—empower yourself every day and intend that your life is a happy one, and is leading you to live your Divine Purpose.

Biography

HelenB—just for Being. Being a mother and grandmother, which I love. Being here at this moment in time, watching life and people, which gives me the inspiration to write my poems.

Being qualified in Massage Therapy, which I passed in my 62nd year, very proud of that! Currently living in London, I have 2 wonderful children Zahra 44, and David 36 and 2 grandchildren, Sean 23, and Amari 5.

I am blessed to have a close relationship with all my family, sister, nephews, cousins and numerous friends who amazingly still love me and give me many moments of joy, laughter and companionship.

I am happily retired—what a Joy! I now have time to "BE ME". To follow my own star, part of which I know is to spread these words around the world for all who would like to read them and, perhaps, find them useful, inspiring, enlightening, and, in some cases amusing!

Angel blessings in abundance.

In Love and Light to you all.

2011

Lightning Source UK Ltd.
Milton Keynes UK
UKOW05f0233200713

214099UK00002B/175/P